Prime Time Rhyme...

This is a work of fiction. Any resemblance to actual persons, living or dead, is purely coincidental.

First Printing Oct. 1990

ISBN# 0-9620467-4-4

Published By: Forward March Inc.
831 Sweeney Ave. Unit G
Redwood City, CA 94063

U.S. Booksellers Distributor: Publishers Group West 1-800-365-3453

Shari's photo by: Mark Lee "Moments To Remember."

Drawing of "The Prince of Rhyme" by: Nancy Maley

Printed in the United States of America

ACKNOWLEDGMENTS

The following poems have appeared, some in slightly altered form, in "Macaroni and Fleas," published by, Fithian Press, Santa Barbara, CA. They are used here by exclusive arrangement:
Farewell, My Pet; Places I'd Rather Be; Roll Call; Where's That Prize?!!; Manners; Harold; Envy; Romeo Finklestein; Brenda; Out, Please; 900 Miles To Texes; Just Me; Roller Coaster; Halloween; Neighbor; Bigger Hugs; Confidence; Hide Me; Sorry; Soory, Doc; Slim; My Bully; Oops!; You Know Who; Unfair Trade; Strange Noise; Lost; Thanks, Guy; 23, 24, 25; Jelly Bean Queen and Chatterbox.

DEDICATION

To Grandma Sophie Mondshane, whose love for children will be remembered, always.

S.C.

To those who feel moody
To those who don't care
To those who think most
Things in life are not fair

These poems may cause you
To think and to cope
To look at the world
With a laugh and new hope

So come share some wisdom
Come spend some time
With the one who knows feelings
The GREAT PRINCE OF RHYME!

OOPS!

I remember a time
When I tried to be cool—
I delivered my speech
While
Sitting
On
A
Tall
Stool
And the class was laughing
But I didn't know why
Because my words
Came out perfect
But I wanted to die,
For as I looked down
I discovered like the rest
That caught in my belt
Was the
Bottom
Of
My
Dress!

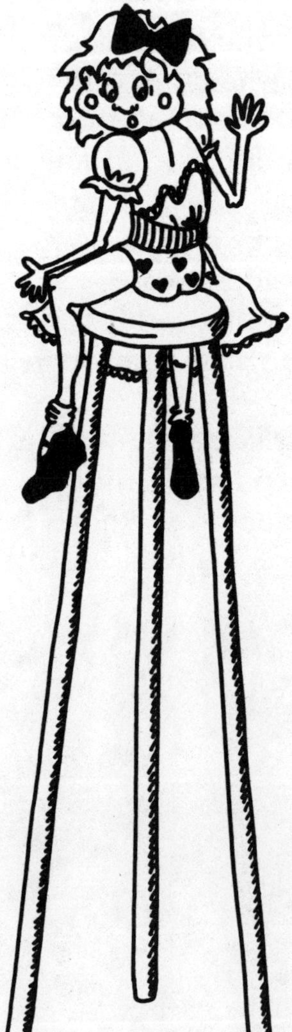

DEAR GOD

Please bless Mom and Dad
And Sue and Frank
Although I know it was Frank
Who broke my bank.

He broke it into pieces
And I happen to know
That he helped himself to money
Which was really low.

Frank, you thief!
How could you?
What a sneaky thing to do.
You lied and tried
To hide it too.

I found pieces in the hamper
Pieces high and low
I should have known
Cuz you were nice to me
Three days in a row.

On second thought, Dear God
If it's all the same to you
Let's make a quick change
and re-arrange
Just bless Mom and Dad and Sue.
Amen!

YOU KNOW WHO

Nine guys up for the team
And who will they pick last?
You know who.

I'm not fast
I'm not slow—
Kind of so-so.

But it never fails,
When it's time to choose,
They won't want
To lose.

It will be really mean
When they pick the team
Because after
            Ralph, Joe,
            Bert, Sam and Moe,
            Larry, Curt,
            And Lou.....
Will be
You know who.

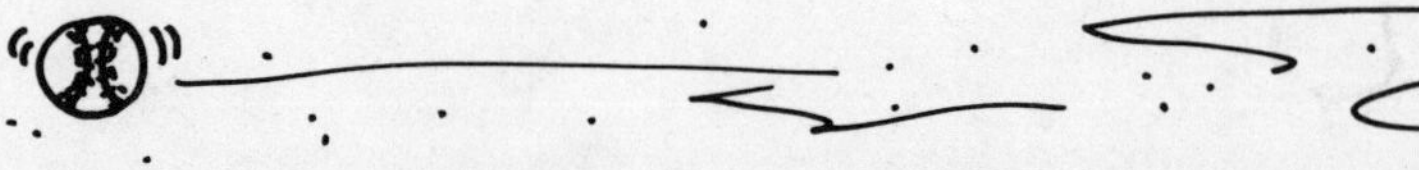

BRENDA

She's rough
Like a Sergeant Marine
Always yelling
"Keep this place clean!"
She's mean.

She's tough
Like a prison guard
"Rake those leaves
In the front and backyard!"

Forever on my case
"Brush your teeth!"
"Wash that face!"
Always preaching
Every rule.
She's cruel.

Sees all
Knows all
Has eyes around her head
And footsteps like lead.

Seven watches up one arm
Each one has
Its own alarm
To make me go to bed on time.
Why couldn't she be
Sweet and kind?
She's rough
She's mean
She's . . . .
Brenda the Babysitter!!

ADAM-DID-IT

ADAM-DID-IT
That's me
Because, you see
When bad things happen
They call for me.
Gum in the rug
Ink on the chair
Jam on the floor
Soap on the stair
Who do they blame?
You'll hear my name
ADAM-DID-IT
That's me.

MANNERS

I know that it's not polite to stare
But there's a strange looking guy
Over there

With earrings and makeup
And orange and green hair

His boots are purple,
With heels stacked high

And he's wearing
A polka dot tie.

The tie has lights
That blink off and on

And his shirt would be nice
But he's not wearing one.

There's a ring on each finger
And one through his nose

A sign on his back that says
"Eat at Joe's"

I know that it's not polite to stare
But there's a strange looking guy
Over there.

900 MILES TO TEXAS

Yesterday we packed
And were ready to go
On our once-a-year trip
To see Grandfather Joe.

The tank was full,
The windows clean—
Eight in the car,
Not an inch in between.

The radio was working,
The tires looked strong—
We were finally leaving!
Not a thing could go wrong.

We yelled to the wind
As our car whizzed past:
"Goodbye House"
"Goodbye Street"
"Goodbye Town"

Oooops! . . .
We had to turn back
Because my big brother Tom
Noticed one small problem.

We forgot mom.

WE FORGOT
MOM!!

23,24,25. . .

Where do you look
When the dentist has his face
Close to yours?
Scraping. . .drilling. . .
Putting in a filling.
Do you count the dots
On the ceiling
Or squeeze your eyes shut tight?
Do you watch his hands
Reach in your mouth
Or do you squint into the light?
Where do you look
When you can't turn side to side,
When your face is stuck
In front of his
And your mouth is open wide?
Do you look into his glasses
And wonder if he knows
That you are busy counting
The hairs up in his nose???

FAREWELL MY PET

My cockroach died today.
I found him belly-up.

Unlucky one
Probably choked on a crumb.

I'll wrap him in tissue,
Lay him to rest,

I'll tuck him away
Where he'll feel the best,

In a cool dark corner
On Mom's second shelf,

Where he used to roam
(When he had his health)

Alongside of the crackers
Behind the white rice—

Goodbye little cockroach!
It sure has been nice.

TOOTH FAIRY

I was drifting off slowly
Just closing one eye
When a vision of beauty
Came floating by.

She stood near my bed
And to tell you the truth
I knew that the Fairy
Had come for my tooth.

Leaning over softly
She gave me a hug
My body lay still while
I stared at the rug.

Her stay in my room
Was not all that long
For the next thing I knew
In a poof, she was gone!

I saw her! I saw her!
I wanted to scream
She paid me a visit
It wasn't a dream.

The magical Fairy
Was unlike any other
And her feet were size 10
Just like my own mother.

The touch of her hand
The feel of her gown
The smell of her hair
It was just like my Mom.

The Tooth Fairy's kid
Was so lucky to find
A Magical Mother
That looks just like mine.

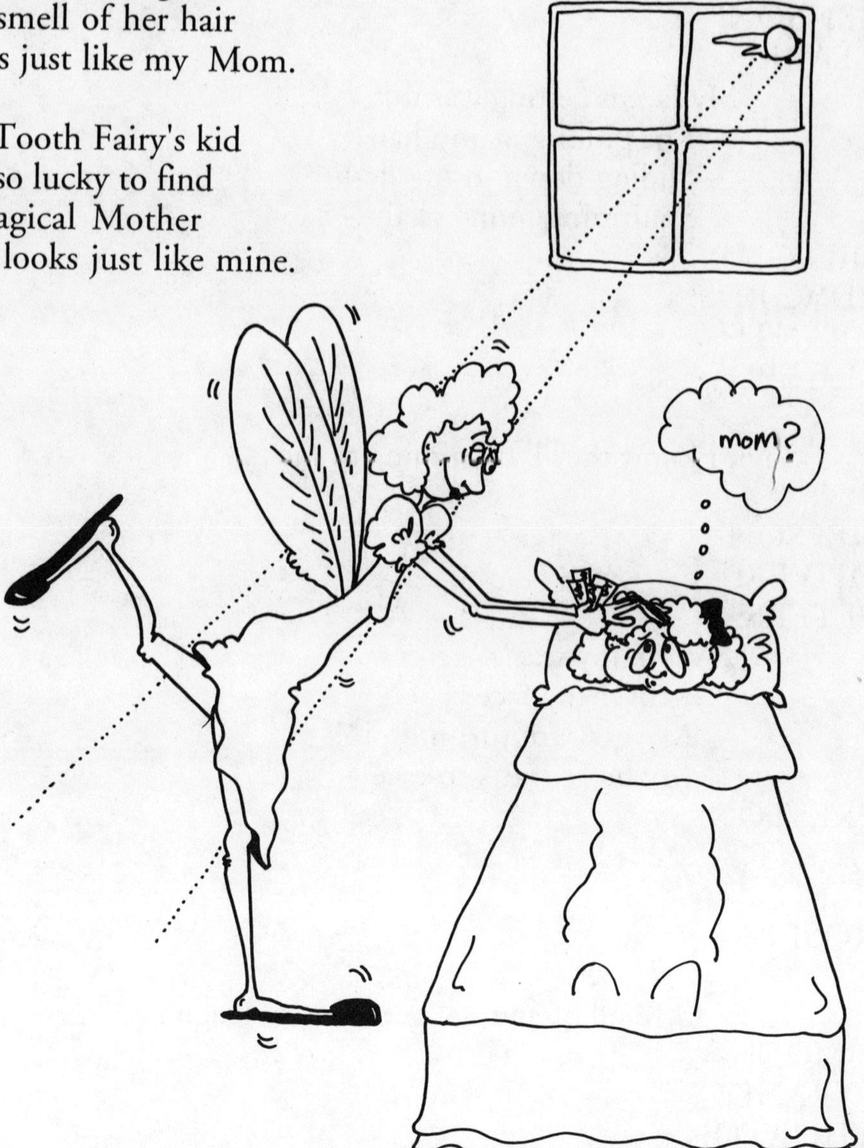

ROLL CALL

ANDERSON!
BENSON!
CLARK!
My face is getting warm
I'm pulling at my hair
Sliding down in my desk
Squirming in my chair . . .
DILLON!
EDWARDS!
GRANT!
McGEE!

Soon I know they'll be coming to me . . .

NELSON!
OLIVER!
PETERS!
Lower in my seat
I cover my face
My ears are turning pink
My heart starts to race
PRESTON!
QUINT!
RAFT!
ROSEN!

O.K. all of you . . . get ready to laugh . . .
SIMON!
STRAND!
THORTON!

. . ."VONSTEINOVICHTERVONTONBERGOWITZ"!!!

Vonsteinovichen von tenbergowitz!!

HIDING OUT

It's a tiny space
But a nice place
To hide . . . I think

Down here
        under
            the sink . . .

Waiting for Mother
To discover the ink
I spilled on her
NEW WHITE MINK!!!

It's a tiny place
behind the pipes
So dark and damp
But at least for now
It's here I'll camp.

INK

TEST

Danny's paper
In plain view
Makes me wonder
What to do
Seven minutes
Left to go
Nothing on
This test I know.
Danny's answers
Clear and neat
Make me wonder . . .
Should I cheat????

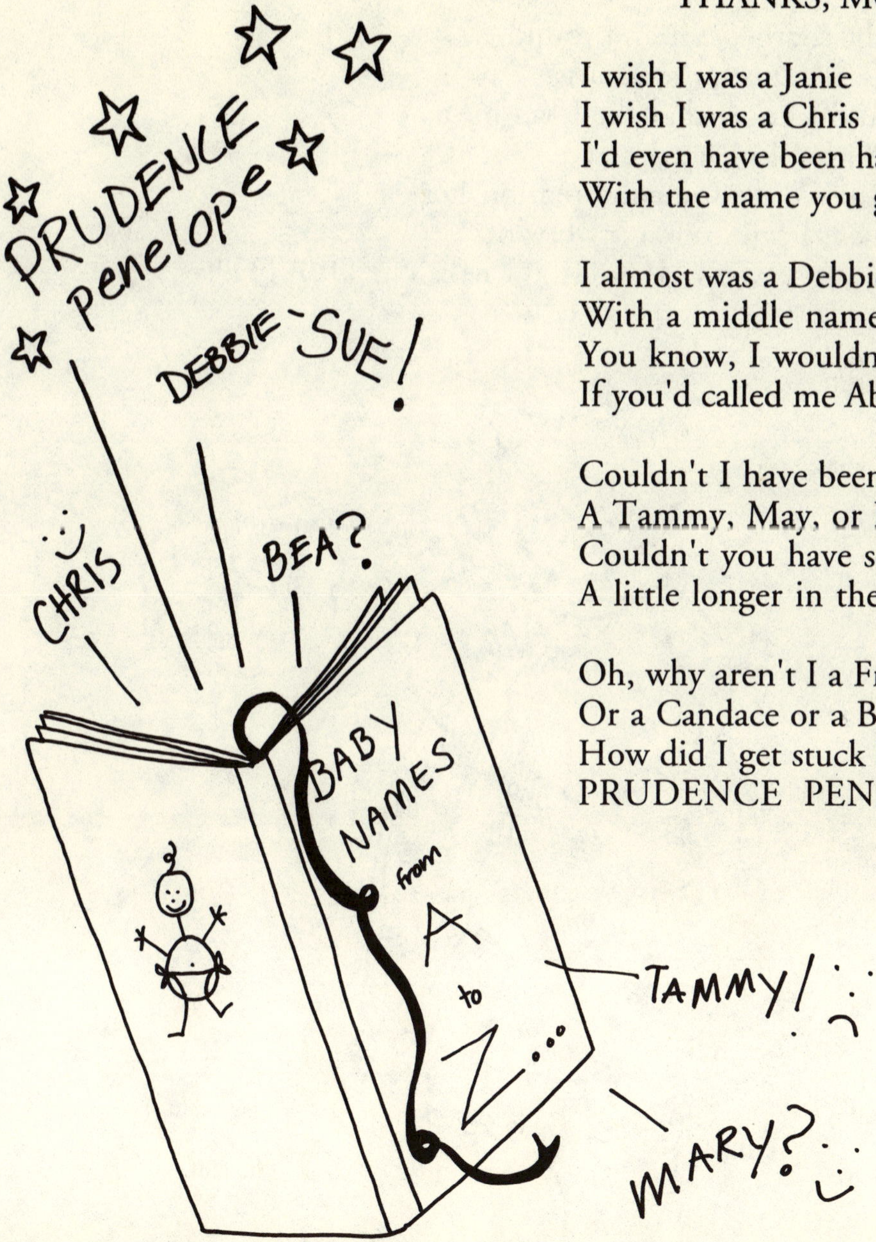

THANKS, MOM

I wish I was a Janie
I wish I was a Chris
I'd even have been happy
With the name you gave my sis.

I almost was a Debbie
With a middle name of Sue—
You know, I wouldn't have minded
If you'd called me Abby Lou.

Couldn't I have been a Lori,
A Tammy, May, or Brooke?
Couldn't you have searched
A little longer in the book?

Oh, why aren't I a Francis,
Or a Candace or a Bea?
How did I get stuck being called
PRUDENCE PENELOPE!!

GRANDMA

She's large, soft and round,
Sweet and quite smart
And I know that she loves me
With all of her heart
But would someone remind her
That I can't catch my breath . . .
Because she's HUGGING ME TO DEATH!!!

LOTS OF DOTS

What are these dots
On my arms and my legs?
What are these dots
On my face and my head?
What are these dots
In my ears and my nose
And what are they doing
Between my toes?
What is this itch
From my hair to my socks
Could it be?
Oh, poor me . . .
I've got
Chicken Pox!!

"STU"

The problem with my friend Stu
Is his LOUD chew
It's not just a nibble
A gnaw
A gulp
Or a munch
But a mind blowing
CRUNCH!

P.S. (Don't ask him to lunch)

BIGGER HUGS

Although I'd never tell her that
I think my Mom's a little fat.
Not huge
Obese
Enormous
Roly poly
Or wide as a tree,
Just overweight
By a pound or three.

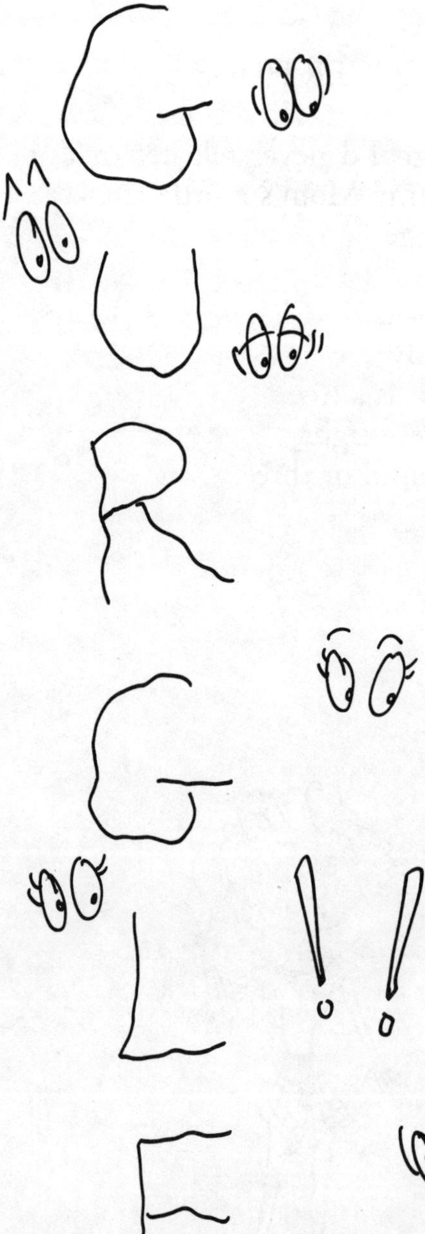

STRANGE NOISE

I was taking a test
The room was still
I was sitting in the back
Between Bobby and Jill
When suddenly, out of the blue
A strange noise was heard
I thought it was Stu
But as I raised by head
My face turned red
For there were 20 pairs of eyes
And they weren't looking at Ted
The class started to whistle
They cheered and . . . yeow!
They asked me to stand
And take a bow

YELLOW YARN

I wonder when she'll notice
That her sweater has no arm
That I have been unravelling
A piece of yellow yarn

It's laying in a pile
Between us on the ground
And comes apart so easily
It hardly makes a sound

I can't seem to stop myself
It isn't very hard
To keep the yarn unravelling
Yard by yard by yard

HALLOWEEN

It's not
That I was scared
I just was
Not prepared
For your visit
Last Halloween

As you know
I didn't
Actually scream
But for the next
Six months
You were in my dream
And so this year
I'm asking
Without sounding
Like a bore . . .

Could you possibly
Skip my door???

OUCH!!

Inching . . .pinching . . .
Moving with care
Hurting . . .pulling . . .
Hair by hair,
The one thing in life
That causes me harm
Is ripping a band-aid
S L O W L Y
Off my arm.

SORRY, DOC

I hope that my doctor wakes up sick tomorrow
With a terrible cold or flu.

I hope the battery is dead
And three tires are flat
And the snow is so deep
That a big giant heap
Will be blocking the street.

Nothing personal, you see . . .

But I hope that tomorrow
My doctor crawls back into bed
With an aching head
And a nose soooo red

That he'll pick up the phone
And call in sick for the day. . . .
Say—I really do like him a lot
But tomorrow is the day for my shot

DOC

TO LOUIS

"Be Mine, Valentine"
the pretty card said
In lace and hearts
Of pink and red.
Cupids floating
Through clouds of white
Lots of glitter
Twinkling so bright.
From which admirer
could this card be . . .
From Martha Jo?
Samantha Lee?
From Cindy Rae
The Irish lass?
From Ann, the smartest
One in class?
From Jill who smiles
From time to time?
Who wants ME
To be their Valentine?
I opened the card
But not very wide
And ever so gently
Peeked inside.
There at the bottom
In a tiny space
Written in pen
Was that happy face
"Surprise Valentine"
and "Have A Nice Day"
from your 4th grade teacher
Miss Edwina McFay!!!

IS VALENTINE'S
DAY

GOTCHA

On a warm humid night
Around the same time
Each year
I hear a familiar noise
Buzzing around my ear
It's Vito
The dreadful
Summer mosquito

SWAT!!
(Missed)

Whizzes by my hair
Circles near my nose
Dives down to
Sit upon my toes

SWAT!!
(Missed)

Flies around my eye
Races to my arm
"Come here little fellow
I'll do you no harm"

SWAT!!

SQUISH

So long, Vito
Guess you're Finito
You dreadful
Summer mosquito!

MISSED

You're moving away TODAY

And I just want to say
That I'll never
Have another friend
Like you—

I'll never laugh
I'll never sing
I'll never play
Another thing
I'll never jump
I'll never run
I'll never have
Any FUN—

I don't know WHAT I'll do
without a friend like YOU.

CHATTERBOX

My family calls me Charles Chatterbox and I
Really don't know why because I like to talk
Just like any other guy unless it's about
Football or baseball or movies or the weather
Or about this cute girl in my class named
Heather or about Science or Math or how much
Water I like to have in my bath and I like
To talk to little kids too and old folks
And strangers although I know there is
Danger in talking to a stranger and it's kind
Of hard when someone says to me "Hi, Charles
How are you?" because I have to tell them
About my cold and my toothache and last week's
Flu and for the next two weeks what I plan to do
And about how I found the . . .

PICTURE DAY

It's picture day at school
And I'm trying to look cool

But my nose is quite runny
My hair sticks out funny
I have three new pimples
A sty on my eye
A splotch on my lip
And I'm not sure why
My braces are gleeming
My cheeks have a rash
The side of my face
Has a two-inch long gash
I feel like a fool

But I'm trying to look cool
Cuz it's picture day at school.

NEIGHBOR

She's old.
I know that she's kind
And she's sweet,
And she wears soft
Slippers on her feet.
I know that she once
Taught school
In a faraway land
And played second clarinet
In a band
And that dozens of men
Kissed her hand.
She walks with two canes,
Her bones are frail,
She shuffles,
Holding on to the rail.
I know that she's kind
And she's sweet
But her hair is white
And her skin is wrinkled
As an old paper kite. . .
She's old.

SHHHHHHHHHH

When I entered the room
I caught by chance
My strange great Aunt
Whispering to her plant
It wasn't just "Hello"
Or "How do you do", but
"Psst . . .?"How are you feeling
Mr. Eddie McGrew?"
"Do you think it might rain?
Will the Rams win the game?
Should I wait for the bus
Or should I take the train?"
I stood and I watched
And was quiet as could be
While my Aunt conversed
With her seven foot tree.

SLIM

Skinny Minnie
They call
After all
What can I say
About how much
I weigh—
62.
So I don't like meat
Or sweets
Or beets.
I hate fruit
And greens
Including beans
And so I guess
I'll stay
Skinny Minnie
After all.

ROLLER COASTER

I'm creeping up the track . . . up toward the sky
And I really don't care to be up this high
Climbing slowly . . . inching up this giant slide

. . . Whooooooosh!!!! Down we go . . .
Mister, can you stop this ride???

Up . . .Up
How can he hear me? He's a dot on the ground
And I'm traveling faster than sound.

We're coming down. . . . .

Maybe if I lean to the side . . .
Whizzzzzz!!!!! We just flew by

Mister, can you stop this ride????
Upside down . . .up and around
I think my stomach just fell to the ground.

Now we're at the top getting ready to drop
I have only one thing to say, Mister . . .

STOP!!

ENVY

She's prettier than me.
Even though I have
Thick blonde curls
That lay in rows
Gathered together
By satin bows . . .
She's prettier than me.
My eyes are bigger
And rounder
And my smile is bright.
I have dimples
No pimples
And my upturned nose
Makes quite a sight.
I have pouty lips
And some freckles to boot
Most everyone agrees
That I'm sooooooo cute
But deep down inside
There's a fact I can't hide . . . .
She's prettier than me.

HIDE ME

My grandmother dressed me today.
She sent me to school
In loud checkered shorts
And a Mickey Mouse belt
And a wide striped shirt
With a collar of felt
A polka dot vest
With buttons that shine
Gray flannel socks
That are one of a kind
High leather boots
With buckles up the side . . .
Even grandmothers should know
That a kid has his pride!

SO LONG

The thunder's going to get me,
Don't laugh, I say it's true.
The rumble's getting closer
In flash of grey and blue.

It's swirling toward my window
With a crack and snap and growl,
I've heard the sound before
It's an evil monster howl.

I know it's going to get me
No matter where I hide
Because it has a million eyes
That can see from every side.

I'm curled up in a ball
In the corner of the room
But I know it won't be long
Before I meet my coming doom

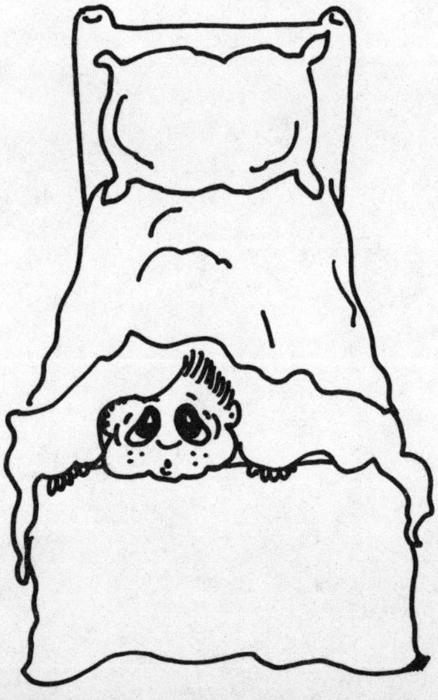

For no matter where I run,
No matter what I do
The thunder's going to get me—
Don't laugh, I say it's true!

FIRST FLIGHT

Silver plane
So fast and free
Flying high
Above the sea
Thunder's rumbling
Lightning's bright
Hope to make it
Through this night
Dipping, gliding
Bumpy air
Engine roaring
Like a bear
At least until
We safely land
Won't someone hold
My little hand?

SORRY

How do you say
"You're not my type"
Without hurting her feelings
Or making her cry
Or having to lie
When you really want to say
That she looks like a fly?

"OH, SOLO MIO"

Windows rattle
Mirrors crack
Bottles shake
Upon the rack
Faucets Rumble
Lights lose power
Father's singing
In the shower!

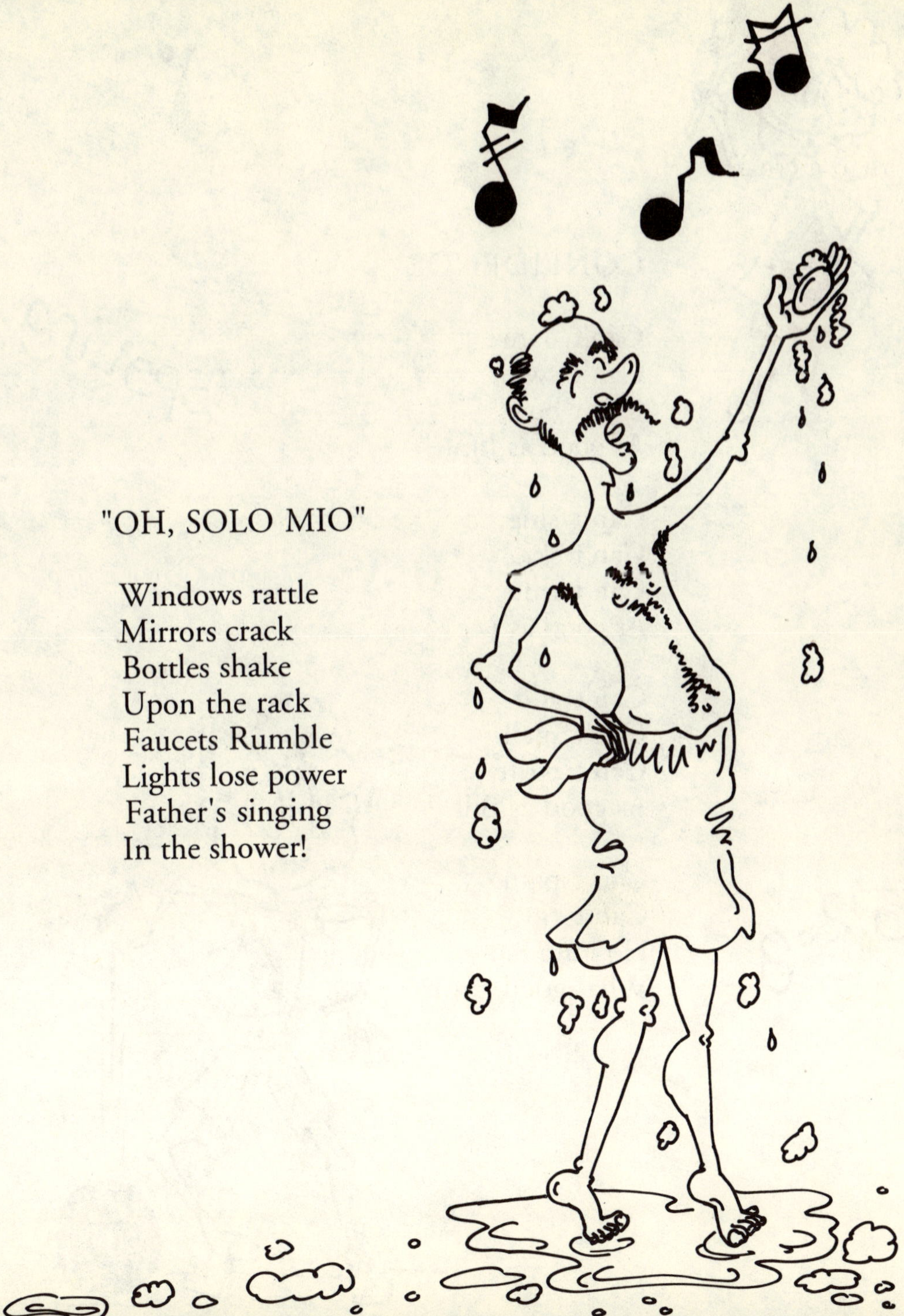

CONFIDENCE

Can't dance
Can't swim
Can't bowl
As good as Jim.

Can't sing
Can't ski
Can't ride
As good as Lee.

Can't add
Can't spell
Can't write
As good as Bill.

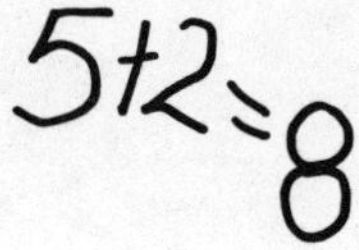

Can't paint
Can't tie
Ho hum . . .
What good am I?

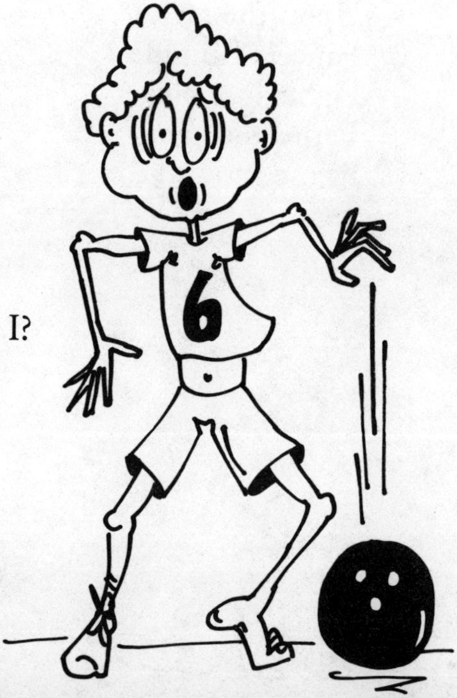

THANKS, GUYS

Worse than measles on the Fourth of July
Or being allergic to blueberry pie
Worse than rats
Or bats
Or shiny new braces
Sunburned faces
Untied laces
Is a fact rather bleak. . .
Today I was crowned
"Geek Of The Week."

I HATE

Asparagus
Spiders
Lightning
Math
Flies
Radishes
My sister Jill
Mice
Weeds
Dirt
Warts
My sister Jill
Squash
Ants
Cavities
My sister Jill
Shots
Onions
My sister Jill
Snakes
My sister Jill
My sister
Jill

PARTY BLUES

If it rains on my birthday
No one will show
I just know.

The grass will be soggy
The sidewalk wet
The ground full of puddles
I bet.

The park will be empty
With slippery slides
Water-drenched rides
And besides . . .

If it rains on my birthday
No one will arrive
And because of the weather
I will never turn 5.

SOMEBODY

Sometimes in the night
When no one can see me
With the sheets pulled tight
I imagine that I am

SOMEBODY. . .

I can predict the future
I have traveled in space
I've discovered a cure
I have won a big race

JANE! JANE!

She saved a baby
From an oncoming train
She found the old man
Who was lost in the rain.

My name is in print
They shake my hand
My face is well known
Throughout the land.

In the night
I am strong . . .

I BELONG . . .

I am SOMEBODY.

JANE WINS!!
GO!
1st
JANE FINDS A CURE!!!
J
Super JANe!

HAROLD

I've tried every trick
To get into the clique

But it's always the same . . .
Just Rick, Mick, and Nick.

Maybe, if
I change my name to VIC . . .

HEAVY FOOTSTEPS

I think Mother will know
It wasn't Ted or Joe
Who ate the batter
Because it is ME
Who is much rounder
And much fatter.
It is ME who ate
The heavy sticky mound
Of sugar and butter
That I accidently found
At around midnight
When no one was awake
It was ME who ate
the glob of dough
For tomorrow's cake.

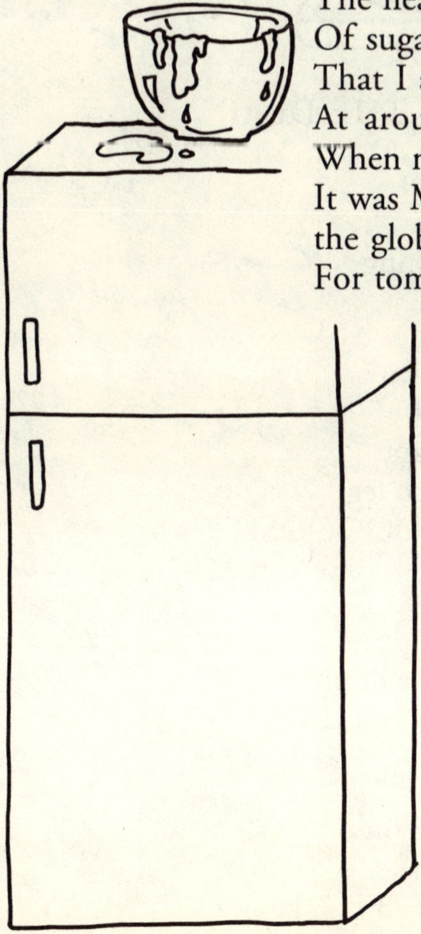

IT CAME FROM THE DRAIN

Just when I went
To Take a drink
I saw a crawly thing
In my sink.

Bulging eyes
Furry head
Antenna ears
A three inch leg.
SWOOOOOOOOSH!!!

Washed it down
Thought it was dead
But up from the drain
Popped it's ugly head.

I think I'll call
My sister to the sink
And have her take
A nice long drink.

OUT, PLEASE

Not that it would happen
But . . .
If this elevator gets stuck
And the lights go out
Would anyone hear my shout?
HELP!!!
If the doors don't open
I have this fear
That no one would hear
My yell for
HELP!!!
Not that it would happen.

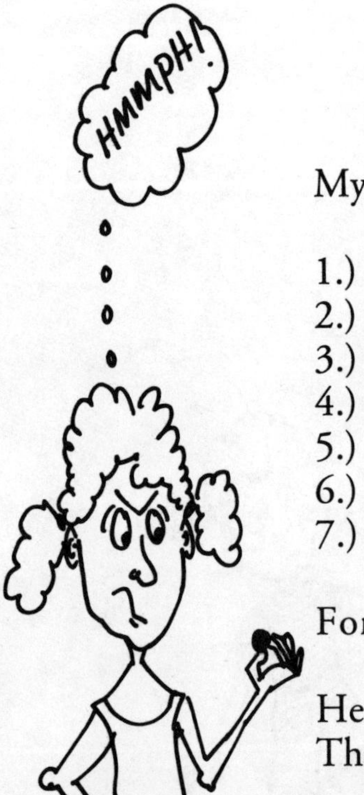

UNFAIR TRADE

My ex-friend Lucy traded me my

1.) Red haired doll
2.) Sixteen pieces of candy
3.) A favorite game
4.) My ballet shoes
5.) A music box with two brass locks
6.) My bracelets and rings
7.) Five other things

For

Her small red rubber ball.
That's all!

MY BULLY

My bully is mean
He chews gum and wears black
He's stupid
And someday I'll tell him that!

My bully has a thick neck
And muscles that bunch
And everyday at school
He steals my lunch. . .

He tells me when to stop
He tells me when to go
He's dumb—
Someday I'll tell him so.

My bully is loud
He's got the biggest mouth in town
When he screams at me
I'm not allowed to make a sound.

He's a jerk
The creepiest guy I've ever met!
And someday I'll tell him
BUT NOT JUST YET. . .

NICE DOGGY

A dog is walking toward me
And he's large.

Should I run
Or walk
Or hide behind that tree . . .
Because he's going to BITE me!

Those teeth
That tail
Closer . . . . .Closer . . . . .
What a mean looking hound.

I'll look the other way
Just walk right by
Hum a silly tune
And pray to make it
Home alive
By Noon.

TIMBER!!!

I'm building a treehouse
It isn't very big
It's taking me forever
Cuz I'm working twig by twig.

It has a small framed window
Leaves upon the floor
Wooden steps that wobble
Right up to the door.

It's tilting toward the neighbors
Swaying in the breeze
I really can't help it but
I think I'm going to sneeze . . .

"Achoooooooooo!!"

I used to have a treehouse
Branches gold and brown—
It's now a bunch of matchsticks
In a pile upon the ground.

ROMEO FINKLESTEIN

It's more than a crush
This warm flush I feel
When I see you
Sitting two rows ahead
Not knowing
Or glancing back once
Or giving a sign
That you care
Or are even aware
Of my great love for you,
Romeo Finklestein

Romeo, oh Romeo,
When will you know
How much I wish that
In another place
In another time
We had met
When you could have been
My Romie
And I, your Juliet.

But for now
I know I'd be content
If you'd just look back
Two rows behind
My dear
My love
My Romeo Finklestein.

XOXOXO,
Frieda Stern

SMILE

Gummy spaces
Left in view
Where my baby teeth
Once grew.

Empty notches
Open spots
What a funny
Mouth I've got.

Sure hope the holes
Fill up in time
At least before
I'm twenty-nine.

JELLY BEAN QUEEN

I'm going to be a teacher
But my very secret dream
Is to wake up one morning
As the Jelly Bean Queen—

To decide on the flavors
To pick the color of the day
To be the first taster
To have the final say—

I know I'll be a teacher
But I still will have my dream
To wake one morning
As the Jelly Bean Queen!

TRUE LOVE

Oh, Marshall . . . .
Is it ME you love?
You call me names
And tug at my hair
When I start to sit down
You pull out my chair
You make weird faces
And once hit me
With your glove
So I'm asking you Marshall . . .
Is it ME you love???

LOST

Today my mom lost me in the store
Two minutes after we walked in the door
And I knew I was in **Trouble**
With a capital **T**
Because the last thing she said
Was directed at me—

Douglas, do not wander away!
O.K. O.K. . .

But I spotted this shelf with some toys
And . . . heck, boys will be boys
So I played for awhile. . .

Well, maybe an hour or two

With trucks and cars that were shiny and new
With knights in armor and baseball cards
Until Mom appeared with a security guard.

Her face was puffy, she was looking really mean
And I said, "Oh hi Mom, where have you been?

. . . . . .Ouch!!!!
It's not fair that my bottom is sore
After all, **SHE lost ME**
In the store

JUST ME

No one to talk to
No one to share
No one to laugh with
No one to care.
No one to swing with
Or sing with
Or do anything with. . .
I guess I'll just hang around
Feeling down.
It's lonely
When you're the new kid
In town.

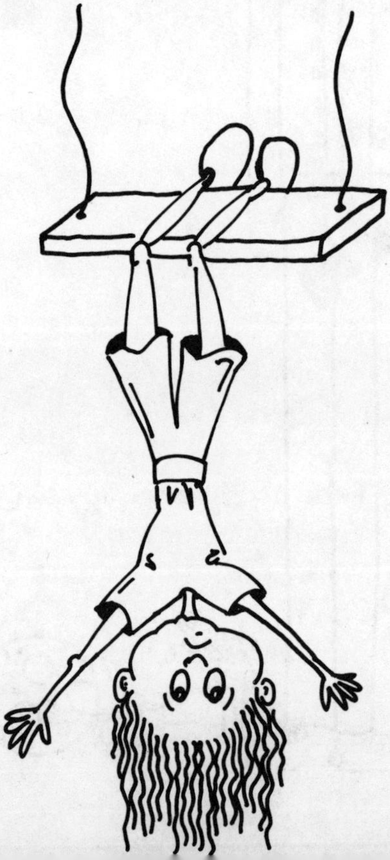

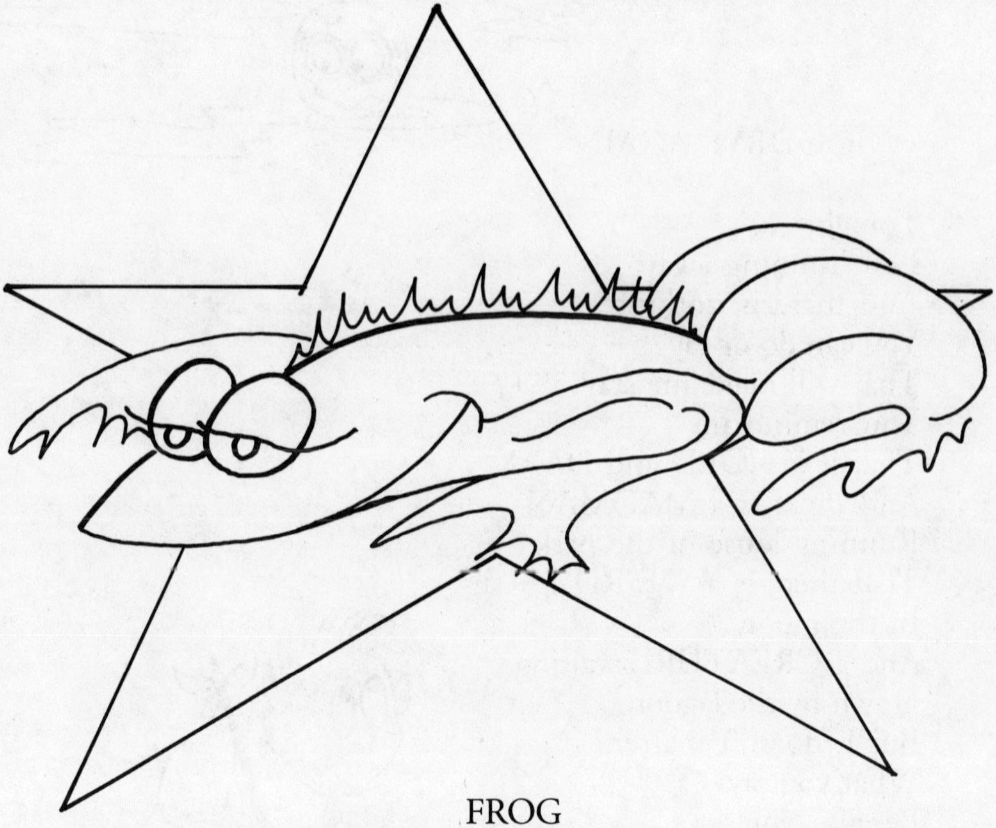

FROG

Wonderful Frog!
I'd like to take you
Home in a jar.
Your eyes are beady,
Your neck hangs down,
Your back is green
With thorns all around.
You're a wee bit ugly
But I'll make you a star—
Come with me,
Let them see
What a wonderful
Frog you are!

GOODBYE AGAIN

Tonight . . . .
I am running away
And there is nothing
You can do or say
That will make me stay.
You remind me
That it is COLD and DARK
And there is a MADMAN
Running loose in the park
That there is a WEIRD FACE
In the moon
And a CREATURE waiting . . .
Down by the lagoon.
But it doesn't matter
What you say
Because, you see . . .
TOMORROW NIGHT
I am running away!

PLATE OF SOMETHING

There's a plate of something
Under my bed
Between two slices
Of stale white bread.
It's greenish, yellowish
Brownish gold
And spotted with mold
From being so old.
Could it have been
Tuna and Mayo?
Cheese and Ham?
Or Peanut Butter
With Strawberry jam?
It's hard to tell what's on that plate
Because it's been there
Since Spring of 1978.

NOT EASY

At fanciful parties
I feel out of place
The thought of being kissed
makes my heart start to race.
I cry about things that
Aren't known to be sad
And sometimes I laugh
When the others are mad.
My temper is fierce
But I wouldn't hurt a flea
As you've probably guessed
It's not easy being me.

BUBBLE GUM

Oh dear, what should I do?
There's a bug in my bubble
And he's stuck in the goo
He's trying to break free
But he can't get through
I dare not pop
I dare not chew
There's a bug in my bubble
What should I do???

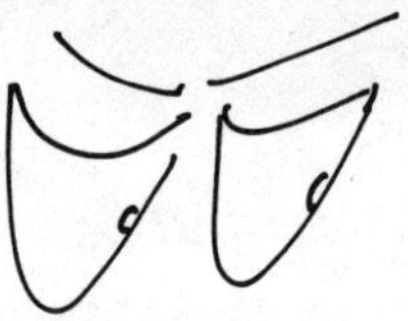

CAMP SPOOKY

Gathered around the campfire
In a haze of smoky light
Telling **S-C-A-R-Y** stories
In the middle of the night.

Dark woods all around us
As **S-P-O-O-K-Y** as can be
Yellow eyes keep blinking
From behind that creepy tree.

B-L-A-C-K-N-E-S-S hangs around us
Like a giant evil dome
Oh . . . . DAD!!!!!
If you can hear me
Can you come to take me home??!!!

WHERE'S THAT PRIZE?

Got to get it
Don't know how
Know I want to
Get it now
Underneath a million O's
At the bottom of
The Cheerios
Feel it . . .grab it
Small in size
Doesn't matter—
GOT THE PRIZE!!!!

INVISIBLE FRIEND

He's always around
When I'm lonely or sad
He stays by my side
When I've done something bad.

He's clever and handsome
Quite tall and quite lean
He likes to eat hot dogs
And pink jelly beans.

It's so fun to chat
with my special friend, Lee . . .
Unfortunately no one
Can see him but me!

ANY PET I CAN GET

I'd like a green lizard
A parrot or a cat
I'd love to have a pony
A rabbit or a bat
I'm hoping for a hamster
A dog to feed a bone
Any living creature
That I could call my own

FAIR WARNING

They say that secrets are for keeping.
That's nice, but where???
Underneath a pillow?
Tucked behind a chair?

Who can keep a secret?—
It sneaks out at every chance
It doesn't have a conscience
Is too hard to hold back—

It runs across the table
It jumps from Steve to Jack
Impossible to keep private
It finds its way to Matt.

A secret can't be hidden
Or kept under lock and key
I know can never keep one
So don't leave yours with me!

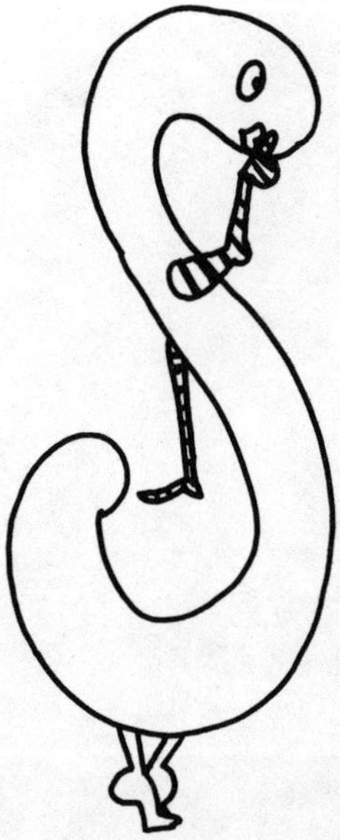

SSHH...
e c r e t
SSHH...

PLACES I'D RATHER BE . . .

At the beach
On the shore
In a shopping mall store
Center row at the show
Or even my house
Out of town
Where I know I'd never be found
Instead of under this tree
Knowing . . .
That in a few short minutes
You will
Kiss me.

DO I CARE?

My friends are mad, you see
And today, no one
Is speaking to me

Do I mind?
Does it hurt?
Am I sad?
Do I look tearful or mad?

Watch me walk
My head held high
Not minding
If they don't say "Hi"

Strolling past . .
Not too fast . . .

Looking like I don't care
My nose stuck up
In the air

Until at last they are gone
And I am . . . alone
To breath a long
Sorrowful
sigh . . .

And cry.

HOT STUFF

My Mother is unlike
any other—

She makes me wear
Scarves and sweaters
And earmuffs— on my knees
Just in case I should freeze

When the temperature outside
Is over 90 degrees!!

LUNCHTIME SURPRISE

I strut past her table
Cool dude that I am
And wink at a pretty
Brunette named Joanne.

Aaaagh!

I've tripped on my sandwich
It's stuck to my shoe
Peanut butter on leather
With jelly gobs too!

Slices of bread
That are soggy and bent
are glued to the bottom
of my shoe like cement.

I reach for a napkin
To rub off the goo
Then find to my horror
The napkin is stuck too!

Everyone is staring
They think I'm a jerk
My face is aflame
I'm going beserk!

Tell me I'm dreaming
This really couldn't be
For how could this happen
To a cool dude like me???

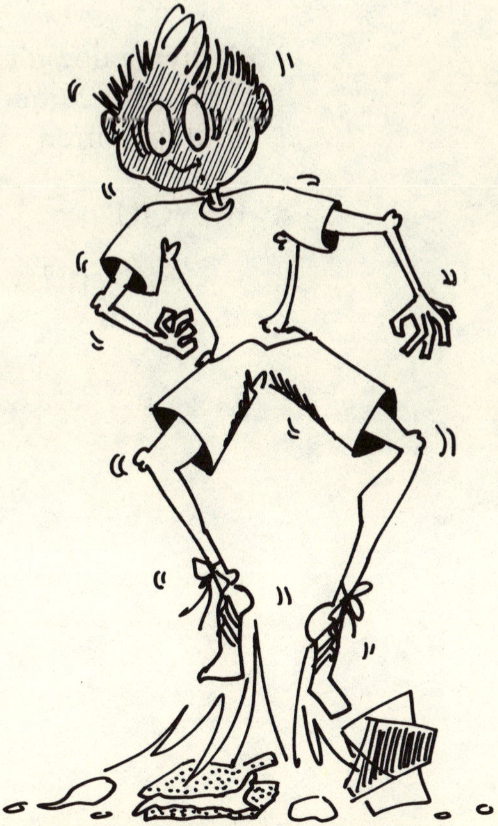

Written by Ms. David's 6th grade class, Parkman Jr. High, Woodland Hills, CA.

RHYMES

A rhyme tells a story
Silly or sad

A rhyme reflects feelings
Happy or mad

Composed in any season
For any reason

A rhyme doesn't have to be
True, if it comes from the heart
And is written

By YOU!

INDEX

If you would like information on ordering additional copies of "Prime Time Ryhme," or other products by Forward March™ Press, please drop us a note or give us a call, we would enjoy hearing from you.

Send inquires to: Forward March™ Press Dept. R
831 Sweeney Ave. Unit G
Redwood City, CA 94063 (415) 366-0708